Adult ADHD

A Guide to Understanding and Managing ADHD in Adults

Table of Contents

Introduction

In a world built for, by, and around neurotypical adults, people with neurodevelopmental disorders often struggle to cope. The onus is always on those on the margins to understand and fit in with a world that makes little sense to them.

The scientific and the psychiatric community do not yet understand much of the intricacies of mental health. For example, ADHD was not recognized as a mental disorder until the 1960s. Research on the disorder has come a long way, but many hurdles are yet to be crossed.

In the United States, 4.4% of adults have been diagnosed with ADHD. Parents of a child with ADHD bear five times more expenses raising their child than parents without them. Today, about 35% of teens with ADHD drop out of school, because they struggle to cope. Likewise, about 51% of teenage girls with ADHD have self-injured. One in four women with ADHD has attempted suicide. 27% of all teenagers in the United States who have a substance abuse disorder have ADHD. 41.3% of adult ADHD cases are severe and, shockingly, severe ADHD cases have been shown to reduce life expectancy by 25 years. For millions of people, understanding their ADHD is the difference between a full, happy life or an unhappy one, stuck in the margins of society.

This book aims to bring help to the 4.4% of adults in the US struggling with adult ADHD. It will provide you with information about the symptoms of ADHD; how you will be diagnosed when you visit a medical professional; how well adult ADHD can be managed; and the self-help and alternative strategies available to you for managing ADHD.

This is not just your first step towards understanding your ADHD. It is also your first step towards regaining your life, happiness, relationships, and your success. This book seeks to reassure you that you are on the right path, while also providing you with scientific research on ADHD to help you better understand the facts about this disorder.

Chapter One: What Is Adult ADHD?

ADHD (Attention-Deficit/Hyperactivity Disorder) is a very common neurodevelopmental disorder. Ongoing in the brain, but manifesting in a person's behavior, ADHD causes inattention and/or hyperactivity-impulsivity that interferes with functioning or development.

If you have ADHD, you will find it tremendously difficult to focus your attention for even short periods. Although you are able to comprehend everything going on around you, your mind wanders off continuously, out of your control. You find it impossible to be persistent in organizing your thoughts. The disorder is also characterized by uncontrollable hyperactivity, where you are constantly moving, talking, fidgeting, or tapping. With ADHD, your body prefers any type of movement to staying still. Since it is uncontrollable, this manifests even at inappropriate times. These uncontrollable movements very often also lead to restlessness and, therefore, physical fatigue.

Also, ADHD is characterized by impulsivity. Impulsivity, as the name suggests, causes you to make hasty decisions and actions without first thinking them through. This often leads to harm. The disorder often causes a desire for instant gratification that can be dangerous to you. As an example, impulsivity could lead to a person with ADHD saying yes to carrying another person's carry-on luggage through the airport, not stopping to think about why another person might ask you to carry out such a strange task.

ADHD symptoms begin in early childhood and continue as a child grows into adulthood. Unfortunately, it is still typical for individuals not to be diagnosed with ADHD until they reach adulthood. Adult ADHD is not too different from childhood ADHD. The treatment is similar (see Chapter Four), as are the symptoms. Likewise, ADHD is harder to recognize in adults than in children because symptoms become less overt. This is usually manifested as a decrease in hyperactivity, but permanent trouble with paying attention, impulsiveness, and restlessness. The severity of these symptoms depends on the individual, with some adults no longer struggling with one or more of the symptoms. Since some adults outgrow it, there is significant difficulty in recognizing and diagnosing the disorder in adults, as opposed to in children.

Adults with ADHD may also struggle with prioritizing their time and responsibilities. This can lead to forgetting important social plans and business meetings or even missing them altogether. An adult with ADHD may face considerable difficulty at work meeting deadlines because of this inability to focus and prioritize. If you have adult ADHD, you may feel uncontrollable impulses, causing you to make hasty decisions out of impatience and to suffer outbursts of anger, frustration, and mood swings. As a downside, this will often affect your personal and professional relationships in quite damaging ways - especially if you are undiagnosed, or the people around you refuse to take your diagnosis seriously.

Adults who remain undiagnosed will have significant difficulty in accomplishing everyday tasks. They may not understand what is wrong or, even, that there is a brain disorder causing their difficulties. ADHD commonly results in mental health problems, especially in patients with severe symptoms. This is particularly true of adults who remain undiagnosed. They may feel as though something is wrong with them because, despite their efforts, they run into significant trouble with appearing "normal" to others. The associated blame and shame can also lead to significant mental health struggles.

ADHD in adults is still a widely studied neurodevelopmental disorder. Contemporary research is still discovering new links between attention-deficit/hyperactivity disorder and trauma, race, emotional dysregulation, and rejection-sensitive dysphoria. Scientific discovery is also championing new, innovative treatments for the disorder, ranging from medication to video games.

Causes Of ADHD

There are a few accepted causes and risk factors for ADHD. Scientists continue to study these causes today to better understand the disorder. By understanding the risk factors and causes, scientists can develop better treatments and management strategies for the disorder. This research study will also enable scientists to understand how to reduce the chances of a person having adult ADHD.

Currently, the exact causes and risk factors of ADHD remain unknown, however, current research has presented a clear link between genetics and the development of ADHD. The National Human Genome Research Institute has been exploring the genetic factors that contribute to ADHD. According to the institute, ADHD appears to run in families, with research studies suggesting that there is a genetic component to the disorder.

This hypothesis was proven correct in 2019 when scientists discovered the first genome-wide significant risk loci for attention-deficit/hyperactivity disorder. It was one of the largest studies on ADHD undertaken at a gene-level scale, with over 55,000 participants from across the world. The study could narrow down hundreds of thousands of human genes to a few genes that may cause ADHD, including DUSP6 and SEMA6D. Dr Anders Børglum, who worked on the study, said:

"These new genetic findings provide completely new windows to understanding the biology behind the development of ADHD. For example, some of the implicated genes influence how brain cells communicate with each other, while others are important for cognitive functions such as language and learning. The risk variants typically regulate how much a gene is expressed, and our results show the genes affected are primarily expressed in the brain."

This research was a breakthrough in the scientific understanding of ADHD because it finally could pinpoint the genetic causes of the disorder. Scientists in the study were elated that research on ADHD could catch up with research on other mental disorders, such as depression and schizophrenia. This new research is a gateway towards allowing scientists to predict the chances of a couple having a baby with ADHD.

Apart from genetic causes, there are other causes that the medical community believes causes ADHD. They are:

- Drinking alcohol and smoking during pregnancy.

- Brain injury, e.g., during contact sports like football.

- Exposure to environmental risk factors like lead or asbestos during pregnancy or at a young age.
- Low birth weight.

- Premature delivery.

Myths about the causes of ADHD, such as overconsumption of sugar, vaccinations, watching too much television, family problems, or other societal issues, like poverty, are just myths. There is no scientific information to suggest any of these risk factors are viable, although they may exacerbate the causes of ADHD. Unlike disorders like depression, ADHD is not triggered by mood swings or mood disorders because of societal or familial problems.

Types Of ADHD

According to the American Psychiatric Association, there are three different forms of ADHD: inattentive type, hyperactive/impulsive type, or combined type. A psychiatrist will usually diagnose what type of ADHD you have based on the symptoms that you have experienced over the past six months.

Chapter Summary

- ADHD is considered a neurodevelopmental disorder.

- ADHD causes inattention and/or hyperactivity-impulsivity that interferes with functioning or development.

- ADHD makes it tremendously difficult to focus your attention for even short periods, causing you difficulties and challenges in normal life.

- Impulsivity from ADHD causes you to make hasty decisions and actions without first thinking them through.

- ADHD symptoms begin in early childhood and continue as a child grows into adulthood. Sometimes children with ADHD outgrow the disorder.

- The causes and risk factors of ADHD remain largely unknown, but scientists recently found a few genes that appear to cause ADHD.

Chapter Two: The Symptoms of Adult ADHD

Spotting the symptoms of ADHD in adults is more difficult than in children because it is easy to blame these symptoms on personal failings.

"My inability to stay focused in the present makes others think I don't care. I get bored quickly and easily, so I struggle with listening to others. In addition, I feel very uncomfortable in group activities where social interaction is required because I prefer not to be noticed. I always feel afraid I will say the wrong thing. Sometimes I even forget to say hello or goodbye, and others accuse me of being rude."

In the above example, it is very easy to mistake the person for just being self-involved and rude, however, difficulty in maintaining relationships is a common symptom of adult ADHD.

Also, it is important to note that you can be diagnosed with other psychological conditions, such as depression, anxiety, and bipolar disorder, even when you have ADHD.

And yet, there is another way to look at ADHD. While it is common for people with ADHD to be looked down on as outcasts and disappointments who couldn't fit into the neurotypical world, there is another side to having ADHD that is rarely celebrated. The symptoms of ADHD, even in the scientific and psychiatric world, are often phrased as though they are nothing but problems. For example, if you have inattentive presentation ADHD, one of your most common symptoms will be phrased as "an inability to stay focused on important tasks". What the phrasing of these symptoms refuses to take into consideration is that ADHD is only a negative in our current world where the workplace is designed for neurotypical people. In many arenas, the symptoms associated with ADHD can actually be of some benefit!

In this way, ADHD differs from many other mental disorders. There is no world in which perhaps the symptoms of depression or constant anxiety are a good thing. However, our neurotypical world is built on long term, ordered, and bureaucratic goals. Therefore, ADHD is considered a *disorder*.

The short-term, concurrent focus of ADHD allows you to be a great problem-solver. Your mind zig-zags from one problem to another; one focus to another. However, this allows your brain to develop thought patterns that can quickly solve problems. The same way you jump from one focus to another, one task to another, one conversation to another, is the same way you jump from one solution to another. While some problems need long-term thinking and long-term solutions, others need short-term thinking. Some decisions need an answer immediately, requiring a brain and a nervous system that can solve problems on the go.

People with ADHD can be very likable people with a sense of humor. Once you are challenged with a problem, you return to that problem until you master it. Your obsession with dominating every new challenge brings innovative solutions to problems. In a neurotypical world of rules and conventions, the ADHD-mind is a limitless resource of innovations that break order and convention for good. As you pour through the symptoms included below, remember that, although you may not be great at taking a 3-hour-long exam or even be able to focus on what people are saying for long periods, it does not mean that there is something "wrong" with you. It simply means that you are a neurodivergent person living in a neurotypical world.

Think of it this way: you are a cat living in a world built by, for, and around dogs. Or to be more scientific, your world is curvilinear, but you are expected to fit into a linear world. In your world, the past, present, and future are never separated; they are not distinct. You live only in the present. Indeed, it is quasi-impossible for you to learn from experience or to look into the future to see the inescapable consequences of your actions. This differs from a neurotypical world where everything is typically divided into a beginning, middle, and an end. With an ADHD brain, there is no beginning, middle, and end. Everything flows on a continuum, rendering you unable to find the beginning or even stick to a point in time. You likely simply jump in the middle and work in all directions at once.

In the following section you will find a list of the different signs and symptoms of ADHD. While you may recognize many of the symptoms in yourself, it is important to never self-diagnose. If you believe you may have ADHD, it's important to consult with a medical professional to receive an official diagnosis, particularly before you begin a treatment plan.

Symptoms Of Predominantly Inattentive Presentation ADHD

You may have predominantly inattentive presentation ADHD if:

- You are easily distracted.

- You find it difficult to pay close attention to details. For example, you may find it impossible to pay attention during long work meetings.

- You make careless mistakes when doing tasks, for example, as a student at college, you may consistently get poor grades because you make careless mistakes in exams. This is because you aren't good at ordination, the ability to plan and do parts of a task in any form of order.

- You avoid (and probably dislike) tasks that need sustained mental effort. This can become a stumbling block in life. For example, you may struggle to pursue certain careers that require sustained mental effort, like engineering or journalism. Preparing reports, completing forms, and even more simple things like following a long recipe can be challenging for you.

- You have problems staying focused on tasks or activities, and long conversations are impossible for you to follow. You may even not seem to listen when someone is speaking to you, as though your mind is elsewhere.

- You do not follow through on instructions, no matter who gives them. You are too distracted and may forget. Or it may demand your sustained focus, which you cannot give, no matter how hard you try. As a result, you may likely not complete schoolwork, chores, or work duties. You may even start tasks but find that you quickly lose focus.

- You have problems organizing tasks and work that you need to do. Organization skills are non-existent for you because your brain cannot process concepts like linearity and linear time. You have poor time-management skills; you are messy and disorganized, even during the most important tasks, and you miss even very important deadlines. Similarly, you very often lose things needed for tasks in your daily life. You often lose things such as your keys, books, glasses, cell phone, medicine, identification documents, and more.

- You forget to do or complete daily tasks. Your chores pile up and your life is held back because you forget to run errands. For example, you do not keep important appointments and forget to go food shopping even when there is no food at home.

Symptoms Of Predominantly Hyperactive-Impulsive Presentation ADHD

You may have predominantly hyperactive-impulsive presentation ADHD if:

- You cannot play, work, or do any activities quietly. As the name suggests, hyperactive-impulsive ADHD makes you hyperactive, so that you cannot stay still. Likewise, you may fidget with things or tap your hands or feet constantly, squirm in your seat, tap your pen, or perform any other action that allows you to release your hyperactive energy.

- You cannot stay seated in one place for even short periods. You always have to be on the move.

- You have difficulty waiting for your turn. You may jump the queue in a coffee shop or feel frustrated when others in front of you in a queue are attended to first.

- You run about or climb objects even during the most inappropriate moments.

- You are always "on the go," as if driven by a motor. This includes constant talking, where it seems you never stop and take a break.

- You blurt out answers even before a question has been finished. For instance, you may finish other people's sentences or overtake conversations, not letting the other person speak.

- You interrupt or intrude on others. You cut into conversations that do not involve you, you forcibly try to include yourself in other people's activities, and you use things without people's permission. Many times, you take over what others are doing.

Combined Type ADHD

Having combined-type ADHD does not signify that your ADHD is more severe compared to predominantly hyperactive ADHD or predominantly inattentive ADHD. It simply means that your symptoms are somewhat evenly distributed between the two different types listed above. If you experience a number of symptoms from both of the aforementioned lists, then this may be the case for you.

Other Common Symptoms Of ADHD

- You may find you have a low tolerance for outside sensory experiences, which is called hyperacusis. The way your brain works causes you to have hyper-heightened senses. For example, you may have to leave the room at the whiff of even the slightest smell, or you may be alert to even the smallest, faintest sounds. Likewise, your thoughts are always in high volume, causing your nervous system to be overwhelmed by day-to-day life experiences.

- You can't screen out sensory input. A neurodivergent person may look at an object, but not be focused on it, or hear what a person is saying without actually listening to it.

- Your mood and energy levels swing from bored, disengaged, or trapped by a task to hyper-focused, energetic, and almost obsessed with a task. When disengaged, you feel lethargic, highly dissatisfied, irritable, and quarrelsome. When super-focused, you are interested, challenged, and happy to start and sustain projects. You can produce high-quality work in a short amount of time when interested.

- Your nervous system never seems to rest. You always search for something interesting and challenging to do. Contrary to the name, "attention deficit", your attention is not deficit (it only becomes deficit when you become bored). Your attention is usually always on "high". You are constantly occupied with your thoughts, which seem to go at a pace of a hundred miles a minute. You typically have a handful of different thoughts in your brain at one time. As a result, you cannot give your full, undivided attention to just one thing, unless you are hyper-focused. (Hyper-focusing will be discussed later).

Why The Symptoms Matter

The symptoms of ADHD are important for medically diagnosing the disorder. Recognizing the symptoms of ADHD is also good for your own mental health. It validates your experience and helps you feel less isolated from others. When you know how your ADHD manifests, you can better manage it.

When you have ADHD, it can feel as though you don't have all the resources you need to survive in the world. Things that seem trivial to most people turn your world upside down in ways that people, subsequently, don't understand. Not only do you feel alienated by the difficulty you face trying to live in a neurotypical world, but you are also further isolated from the world when people misinterpret your actions, trivializing them as rude, clueless, ignorant, arrogant, high maintenance, demanding, irritable, and odd. You may have tried to "fit in" and failed woefully. What is normal to you is just not normal to others and you are often singled out as "different".

Fortunately, you cannot run away from your symptoms. I say, fortunately, because you are perfectly normal as you are. You do not need to be neurotypical to be "normal". You simply need to understand yourself better so that you can learn how to function to your best abilities in the current world. Understanding yourself will also help you learn how to use ADHD's advantages to the fullest and how to minimize the problems that ADHD may bring. Without full knowledge of the symptoms of ADHD, you may begin using maladaptive techniques to thrive.

Chapter Summary

- Spotting symptoms of ADHD in adults is more difficult than spotting symptoms of ADHD in children.

- You can be diagnosed with other psychological conditions if you have ADHD.

- People with ADHD can be very likable people with a great sense of humor.

- People with ADHD often find innovative solutions to problems.

- It is important to never self-diagnose. If you believe you may have ADHD, seek a diagnosis from a medical professional.

Chapter Three: How ADHD Is Diagnosed in Adults

Diagnosing ADHD is very important for your long-term happiness. When left undiagnosed or untreated, adult ADHD often comes with comorbidities, such as anxiety, PTSD, depression, and eating disorders.

ADHD cannot be diagnosed with a lab test. There's no single test for ADHD. Instead, a qualified professional will diagnose it by gathering information from you about your behavior, your thought processes, and the struggles you encounter in your daily life. A comprehensive evaluation usually incorporates a review of past and current symptoms and the use of adult rating scales or checklists. Fill out a checklist and have a medical evaluation (including vision and hearing screening) to first ensure that the symptoms are not because of other medical problems. Your medical practitioner will have to gather information from you, such as your current medical issues, personal and family medical history, and the history of your symptoms, starting from the beginning of your symptoms in childhood.

Diagnosing ADHD in adults can be complex because many undiagnosed adults have learned to hide or mask many of their symptoms over the years. Some medical conditions and treatments may also mimic signs and symptoms of ADHD. For example, drug use and misuse, like alcohol misuse and the use of medically diagnosed drugs can cause many similar symptoms. Likewise, mental health disorders, such as depression, psychiatric disorders, and anxiety may also mimic symptoms of ADHD, as do other medical problems that affect thinking and behavior. If you have sleep disorders and brain issues, hypoglycemia (low blood sugar), and other developmental disorders, it is possible to mistake their symptoms for ADHD also.

Learning Your Personal History

The medical professional will ask you a lot of questions about your childhood. ADHD begins in childhood, so the professional will need to find out your childhood symptoms. They will need to know things such as:

- Did you frequently get in trouble at school?

- Were you disorganized throughout your childhood?

- Did you get poor grades or good grades in school?

- Were you called words like: "lazy", "messy" or "careless"?

- Did you feel misunderstood at school and isolated at school or home?

When you go in for your diagnostic appointment, you might like to take in your report cards and other records of your school days, if you still have them or can find them. Report cards will have not just your grades, but teacher comments about your personality, character, and behavior that can point towards your symptoms of ADHD. You should also take in your medical records. If your parents or guardians have taken you in to see a medical professional during your childhood, these records can also point towards symptoms of ADHD, even if you were misdiagnosed at the time.

The professional evaluating you may also ask to contact a parent, guardian, former principal, childhood psychiatrist, or anyone else who can share information about your childhood. You may feel anxious if you cannot recall some childhood experiences. This is common, so do not worry. The professional will not diagnose you with ADHD unless you have shown symptoms of the disorder before the age of twelve. It's tough to recall events that happen to you before the age of twelve, so feedback from adults around you at the time is very important. Some symptoms you present may have changed as you matured, but this does not mean you necessarily no longer have ADHD.

Evaluating Your Symptoms/Behavior Today

Your childhood history will be followed by an evaluation of your symptoms today, including any difficulties or troubles you've had as an adult because of these symptoms. Your medical practitioner will probably ask you some version of the following questions:

- Do you feel misunderstood at work and isolated from your loved ones and colleagues?

- Do you often forget to pay your bills or attend important appointments and meetings?

- Do you struggle with focusing on or completing college studies or work tasks?

- Do you face considerable difficulties in your relationships?

To diagnose ADHD, a professional has to determine that the symptoms that you experience are causing you deep difficulty.

Subsequently, if you have multiple symptoms of ADHD, but they cause you no difficulties, you won't be diagnosed with ADHD. Therefore, this stage of your diagnosis is very important.

You should share everything with the professional. Be honest, even if you feel embarrassed or feel it is not relevant. The professional will most likely require that some other people in your life fill out a questionnaire about your behavior and character. No matter how good we may be at self-reflection, we all have blind spots in our character. Those close to you will see symptoms and behavioral issues that you may have missed. They bring a different point of view to experiences that will help the professional paint a full picture of your symptoms. As an example, you might think you have mastered the art of friendly conversation, but a friend might believe that you act very bored when others are speaking to you about a topic you have no interest in.

In addition, an ADHD diagnostic procedure usually involves one or more behavior rating scales. Typically, a rating scale contains between 20 to 90 questions that evaluate the frequency of ADHD-related behaviors. The questions are always designed based on the Diagnostic and Statistical Manual of Mental Disorders (DSM-5) definition of ADHD.

add.org has a good example of a behavior rating scale. You can find the Adult ADHD Self-Report Scale at: https://add.org/wp-content/uploads/2015/03/adhd-questionnaire-ASRS111.pdf.

You might be asked to fill out the scale before the evaluation or to complete it during the appointment. These scales will not give you a complete diagnosis on their own, neither will they give you sufficient, objective medical evidence. No matter what rating scale you use, the scale will always be subjective. They are still very beneficial because they help paint a clearer picture about your symptoms.

There are four scale types used to diagnose ADHD in adults:

- Adult ADHD Self-Report Scale (ASRS v1.1).

- Adult ADHD Clinical Diagnostic Scale (ACDS) v1.2.

- Brown Attention-Deficit Disorder Symptom Assessment Scale (BADDS) for Adults.

- ADHD Rating Scale-IV (ADHD-RS-IV).

Despite the different rating scales, they all will require you to answer questions on behaviors such as:

- Your experiences with squirming.

- Your experiences with having difficulty focusing, organizing, and paying attention.

- Your experiences with fidgeting.

- Any difficulties following through on instructions or tasks.

- Any difficulties you have being patient.

- Any difficulties staying still.

- Any difficulties with being unable to wait your turn.

- Any difficulties interrupting others.

- Any difficulties remembering appointments or obligations.

Checking For Other Mental Health Conditions

Some medical professionals will also want to test you for other mental health conditions. For instance, you may need cognitive testing that identifies learning or intellectual disabilities which cause difficulties at college or work. A mental health test will also test for personality or mood disorders. Some of these personality disorders mimic symptoms of ADHD. These tests are a fail-safe to make sure that your symptoms are not caused by other mental or personality disorders, making your ADHD diagnosis accurate.

ADHD does not cause other psychological or developmental problems. However, other disorders often present themselves once you have ADHD, further complicating the treatment of the disorder. These typically are:

Anxiety Disorders

Anxiety disorders are fairly common in adults with ADHD. Anxiety disorders are characterized by intense anxiety, worry, and nervousness about a plethora of things, including personal health, work, social interactions, and everyday routine life circumstances. When you have ADHD, your anxiety can be made worse by the challenges and difficulties caused by ADHD.

Mood Disorders

Depression, bipolar disorder, or another mood disorder are very common among people with ADHD. Mood disorders are not directly caused by having ADHD. However, they can be worsened by the symptoms of ADHD, including repeated failures and frustrations; the misunderstandings that others have towards your symptoms; and your inability to connect emotionally with other people.

Other Psychiatric Disorders

Adults with ADHD have a greater likelihood of developing other psychiatric disorders, such as substance use disorders, personality disorders, and intermittent explosive disorder.

Learning Disabilities

As discussed in an earlier chapter, adults with ADHD usually perform badly on academic testing, scoring lower than someone of the same intelligence, education, and age. Learning disabilities are often characterized by trouble understanding and communicating.

Finding A Professional to Diagnose ADHD

Finding a mental health professional or physician to diagnose you for ADHD can be a challenge, but don't be anxious. The following tips will help you find a professional with no hassle:

- Book an appointment with your primary care doctor to get some recommendations.

- Speak with your therapist (if you have one) about professional recommendations.

- Use the internet to search for professionals in your local or regional area. Try to find reviews of these professionals or ask around to hear word-of-mouth reviews.

- Research who (and what services) your insurance will cover.

- Don't be afraid to ask questions. Likewise, don't be afraid to try several professionals until you find someone that you're comfortable with.

Chapter Summary

- When left undiagnosed or untreated, adult ADHD often comes with comorbidities, such as anxiety, PTSD, depression, and eating disorders.

- There's no single test for ADHD. There are a few tests you may have to take in order to be accurately diagnosed with ADHD.

- Your doctor may need to question your family members and former authority figures to diagnose you with ADHD.

Chapter Four: How Adult ADHD Is Typically Treated

After you are diagnosed with ADHD, the next step towards managing your ADHD is seeking treatment. Treatment will help you immensely. Diagnosis is often the turning point for those with adult ADHD. Many people with adult ADHD often report that this is the first time they feel "normal" in their lives after years of dealing with crippling pain, sometimes through maladaptive strategies like drug abuse.

Thus, once the shame and the uncertainty are taken away by diagnosis, the next step towards healing is treatment. Treatment will help you stop the detrimental symptoms, such as your inability to focus on a project that does not interest you, and improve the beneficial symptoms, such as your ability to hyper-focus on a project that does interest you.

Many people diagnosed with adult ADHD say the same thing: treatment helped them release all the tension, pain, and misunderstanding of the previous few decades. In return, they could gain more happiness and contentment about who they are.

The treatment for ADHD can be medicinal, therapeutic, or a combination of both. The type of treatment that works for you will depend on whether you have mild or severe ADHD, the type of ADHD you have, and the type of symptoms that you present. Whether you are prescribed medicinal or therapeutic methods, it is important to note that your treatment is not a cure, but a tool inside a specialized toolbox for building an ADHD-friendly life. Every form of treatment is a different type of tool for building a life specific to you.

Typically, however, your doctor or psychiatrist will prescribe one or more of these treatments:

Medication

For a while, Ritalin and Adderall were the most popular drugs associated with ADHD. These drugs were so popular that it became widely believed that these were the only treatments available for ADHD (known as ADD in the past). This is, of course, untrue. Medication does not work for everyone. Where it is successful, it does not target all the symptoms of ADHD. Remember that medication is just one of many safe and effective treatments that work as tools in your toolbox; some tools, although effective for others, won't work very well on your own symptoms. This is perfectly normal.

For people who can use medication on their symptoms successfully, medication helps to improve attention and concentration. Other symptoms like forgetfulness, procrastination, poor time management, and disorganization are not helped by medication. As these are very pertinent symptoms affecting people with ADHD, you will need other "tools" to help you improve these symptoms. Medication works very well when combined with other treatment options. You will enjoy the benefits of your medication much better if you supplement it with other treatments that address emotional and behavioral issues and treatments that teach you well-adjusted coping skills.

As with all other medications for all other disorders and illnesses, every individual will react differently. On the one hand, you may experience little to no relief while another person with ADHD experiences dramatic improvement. Likewise, the side effects of ADHD medication differ from person to person. For some people, the side effects of medication outweigh the benefits. It is impossible to tell how one individual will respond to medication, so be prepared to spend a "trial" period finding the right medication and dose that works for you. It is also possible for your medical history to limit your treatment options. Your doctor will ask you about your medical history to get an idea of which of the following drugs will probably work best for you and which ones may pose a risk to your health.

Some medications which you may be prescribed include:

Stimulants

Stimulants are the most commonly prescribed drugs for ADHD. They are typically the first course of drugs used to treat ADHD. Your doctor will likely prescribe you a central nervous system (CNS) stimulant, which works by increasing the amount of norepinephrine and dopamine in the brain. Norepinephrine and dopamine are hormones and neurotransmitters. Neurotransmitters carry information between neurons in your central nervous system. By increasing the amount of dopamine and norepinephrine, you are empowering your CNS to carry more information than it previously could. Subsequently, your concentration improves and your fatigue (caused by trying to concentrate) reduces.

There are many generic versions of stimulants, so you don't have to worry about high costs. Some stimulants are only available as more expensive brand-name versions, however.

Stimulants typically come with some negative side effects, including suppression of appetite, weight loss, sleep disturbances, abdominal pain, and headaches. Other side effects can include anxiety, dry mouth, dizziness, dyspepsia, emotional irritability, fatigue, nausea, fever, vomiting, and nervousness.

If you overdose on stimulants, the levels become toxic, causing stimulant excitation that can lead to stroke, heart attack, seizures, or even fatal overheating. You can also have serious side effects, which comprise of stimulant addiction, infection, serious allergic reaction, tachycardia, psychotic episodes, rhabdomyolysis, cardiomyopathy, prolonged erections, Stevens-Johnson syndrome, and toxic epidermal necrolysis.

Commonly prescribed stimulants include the following:

Methamphetamines (Desoxyn)

Methamphetamines work by stimulating the central nervous system. Scientists are still baffled about how they work to help improve ADHD symptoms. What is known, however, is that they increase the amounts of hormones like dopamine and norepinephrine in your brain.

Methamphetamines come as an oral tablet to be taken once or twice daily.

Methylphenidate

Methylphenidates block the reuptake of norepinephrine and dopamine in your brain, helping to increase levels of these hormones. As a stimulant, it comes in immediate-release, extended-release, and controlled-release oral forms. You can also get it as a transdermal patch, packaged under the brand name, Daytrana. Methylphenidates can come as generic versions or more expensive brand-name versions. Some of the brand-name versions you can get include:

- Aptensio XR (generic version available)

- Metadate ER (generic version available)

- Concerta (generic version available)

- Daytrana

- Ritalin (generic version available)

- Ritalin LA (generic version available)

- Methylin (generic version available)

- QuilliChew

- Quillivant

You may also be prescribed Dexmethylphenidate, another stimulant that improves ADHD symptoms. Dexmethylphenidate, as the name suggests, is like methylphenidate. It is available under its brand-name version, Focalin.

Amphetamines

There are different amphetamines, including:

- Amphetamine: Amphetamine is not available as a generic version. It comes in brand names known as Evekeo and Adzenys XR-ODT. They come as an oral tablet, extended-release orally disintegrating tablet, and an extended-release oral liquid.
- Dextroamphetamine: Dextroamphetamine comes as oral tablets, oral extended-release capsules, and oral solutions. It is a generic drug with no brand-name version.

- Lisdexamfetamine: Lisdexamfetamine comes as an oral capsule and an oral chewable tablet. It comes only as a brand-name drug, Vyvanse.

Amphetamines either come in immediate-release form, to be released in your body right away and extended-release oral forms, to be released into your body slowly. They are available as brand names and generic types. The brand names for these drugs include:

- Adderall XR

- Dexedrine

- Dyanavel XR

- Evekeo

- ProCentra
- Vyvanse

Stimulants can be very effective in keeping your thoughts organized and helping you pay attention and stay focused.

Unfortunately, many people become easily addicted to the drug's effect on the brain, causing serious problems for them.

If you want to avoid the negative side effects of stimulants, particularly addiction, you can ask your psychiatrist about nonstimulants.

Nonstimulants

Nonstimulants work on the brain differently than stimulants do. Although nonstimulants affect neurotransmitters, they don't do so by increasing your dopamine levels. They work more slowly so that you don't see instant results. Rather, it takes longer to see results from these drugs.

If stimulants are not effective on you or they are not safe for you, your doctor will prescribe you nonstimulants. The different nonstimulants include:

Atomoxetine (Straterra)

Unlike stimulants which release more norepinephrine into your brain, Atomoxetine (Strattera) blocks the reuptake of norepinephrine in your nervous system. This allows norepinephrine to work longer.

It comes as an oral form you take once or twice per day and is also available as a generic brand.

Atomoxetine has caused liver damage in a few users. Watch out for signs of liver problems while taking Atomoxetine. Indeed, your doctor will check your liver function regularly when you are on this drug.

Signs of liver problems you must watch out for are:

- A swollen or tender abdomen.

- Jaundice (yellowing of the skin or of the eyes).

- Fatigue.

Guanfacine ER (Intuniv)

Guanfacine is typically prescribed for high blood pressure in adults but is often prescribed for ADHD in adults too. It has been shown to help some adults with their memory and behavioral problems, aggression, and hyperactivity.

It is available as a generic version and as a time-release version called Guanfacine ER (Intuniv).

Clonidine ER (Kapvay)

Clonidine ER (Kapvay) reduces impulsiveness, hyperactivity, and distractibility in adults with ADHD. Like Guanfacine, there are other forms of clonidine that are used to treat high blood pressure in adults. Since it lowers blood pressure, you may feel light-headed when you take it. Clonidine ER (Kapvay) is available as a generic brand.

Nonstimulants rarely cause agitation, sleeplessness, fatigue, or suppression of appetite. This is because they have a longer lasting and more "steady" effect than most stimulants. Stimulants typically take effect and wear off abruptly. Consequently, nonstimulants don't pose the same risk of abuse or addiction. There are, however, side effects caused by nonstimulants.

Clonidine (Kapvay) and Guanfacine (Intuniv) can sometimes cause headaches, sleepiness, fatigue, sedation, and dizziness. Be careful when using Clonidine (Kapvay) and Guanfacine (Intuniv) if driving or using heavy machinery because they cause drowsiness. Atomoxetine may cause a loss of appetite, weight loss, fatigue, nausea, mood swings, and upset stomach. Although rare, Atomoxetine can also cause jaundice and liver problems, suicidal thoughts, long-lasting erections, and serious allergic reactions. On rare occasions it can cause low blood pressure and changes to your heart rhythm.

You and your doctor must monitor the side effects of all medications that you take for ADHD. If medication for ADHD is not carefully monitored, it becomes much less effective and can even become risky and fatal.

Treatment for ADHD does not have to only be in the form of pharmaceuticals. Any action you take to manage or reduce your symptoms is a form of treatment. Of course, you will always need professional help along the way, for instance, you will need professional psychiatric help if you choose therapy. However, you still have plenty of agency in choosing what types of treatments you want to try. Remember that you want to build an ADHD-friendly life and medication is just one part of this new life. Chapters Five and Six will teach you the different ways you can treat your ADHD alongside using medication.

Chapter Summary

- After you are diagnosed with ADHD, the next step towards managing your ADHD is seeking medical treatment.

- Treatment will help you stop the detrimental symptoms of ADHD.

- Every form of treatment for ADHD is a different type of tool for building an ADHD-friendly life specific to you.

- Stimulants are the most commonly prescribed drugs for ADHD.

- Be prepared to spend a "trial" period finding the right ADHD medication that works for you.

- Nonstimulants work on the brain differently than stimulants do.

Chapter Five: How Well Can ADHD Be Managed in Adults?

Adult ADHD can make life very difficult for you when not treated. Indeed, ADHD has been linked to:

- Unemployment (or being unemployable).

- Poor school (college) or work performance.

- Alcohol and substance misuse.

- Poor self-image.

- Suicide attempts.

- Unstable, unfulfilling relationships.

- Financial problems.

- Trouble with the law.

- Frequent car accidents or other accidents.
- Poor physical and mental health.

As you can see from the above list, ADHD can lead you to very dark and unsavory places in life, if left unmanaged. For instance, dealing with poor self-image can lead to other more serious mental and mood disorders, such as depression and extremely low self-worth.

When you have ADHD, you can still self-regulate when negative behaviors, thoughts, and emotions threaten to overwhelm you and others around you. With self-regulation, you can keep the more self-destructive behaviors in check. Some good ways to self-regulate include:

For Focus

- Take easily accessible notes during meetings and lectures. For example, you can take handwritten notes or record all your notes. Afterward, you can fill in the details before you forget.

- Take brief breaks to prevent yourself from getting bored. It is easier to focus on tasks for longer periods when you are not bored. You can do some stretches, make a nice healthy meal, or do some exercise to boost your brain health.

- Divide up large tasks into smaller, more manageable ones that take less time. Reward yourself after you complete each task. For example, a small sweet after each task.

For Distractions

- Work in areas where there are fewer distractions. If you are at work or the library, request a private work or study area, where there are few distractions or noise.

- Set aside set times during the day to return phone calls and emails. Allow your calls to go to voicemail until the set time. That way, you are not distracted by answering calls or returning phone calls throughout the day.

- Use headphones to drown out office noise. You may play soft music to help keep your concentration.

For Organization

- Automate all your online payments of bills. This way, you don't forget to pay them.

- Keep a notebook and write your to-do tasks in it. If you have a smartphone, keep a to-do list on your smartphone. Always update your to-do list immediately once a task is completed.

- Put appointments on your phone and set up alarm reminders before the event. If you have a paper calendar, mark deadlines on calendars as a visible reminder tool. You can also use daily planners or online task organizers that will help you keep track of tasks and events.

- Complete important tasks before moving on to the next one. Take regular breaks while completing important tasks to help you maintain focus.

- Start your day with a mindfulness practice and a quick stretch to clear and refresh your mind. Then spend 20 minutes afterward organizing your tasks for the day.

- To prevent losing important items, designate specific areas to place specific important items, like keys and wallets. Keep a routine of placing these items in these designated spots so you don't lose anything. Trying to find things you misplaced can further disorient you when trying to keep to a set routine.

- Keep sticky pads around the house and around your workspace to jot down important notes. Place these notes in areas where they are highly visible, like on the fridge door.

- If you are using a filing system at work or home, label everything and color-code folders or tabs.

Exercising

Regular exercising is a great way to manage the symptoms of ADHD. Exercising naturally releases dopamine and norepinephrine, the two neurotransmitters that stimulant medications help to produce in patients with adult ADHD.

Regular exercise increases your mood, memory, concentration, focus, and motivation. As well as dopamine and norepinephrine levels, exercise boosts your serotonin levels. The increase of all three neurotransmitters improves your focus and attention. Regular exercise affects you in similar ways that your medication does - without the side effects. For instance, regular exercise has been shown by research to be just as effective as prescription medication for easing mild depression. Similarly, by burning extra energy through regular exercise, you can decrease your impulsivity levels.

A combination of regular exercise and medication will help you significantly reduce your negative ADHD symptoms, so try to exercise at least 4-5 times a week. You don't have to go to the gym to exercise. A simple 30-minute walk will provide your body and central nervous system with significant benefits. If you can do more heart-pounding exercises, like a fast run or burpees, this will help you too. However, always pick an exercise that you enjoy so that exercise does not become a chore for you.

Last, you might like to incorporate some horticultural therapy into your exercise. Horticultural therapy is the use of plants or plant-based activities to feel good. Here, it means going for a walk in the park or the woods or doing some yoga outdoors. We will discuss horticultural therapy further in Chapter Six.

Sleeping

Sleeping is as important as food, water, and air for us humans. Every one of us benefits from it. When you have ADHD, poor quality sleep often serves to worsen your symptoms. You want to get a good night's rest every night. Improving the quality and quantity of your sleep will likely improve your attention, focus, and mood.

To get better sleep, practice yoga and meditation an hour before bed every day (see Chapter Six for a discussion on meditation and yoga as a self-help strategy). This will also help you to stick to a set bedtime every day. By creating this routine, you will naturally get sleepy around the same time every night. Always sleep in a completely dark room and avoid caffeine during the afternoon and night hours.

One of the side effects of your medication could be difficulty falling or staying asleep. If you try the above methods and are still having difficulties, speak with your doctor about your worries.

Eating Healthily

Eating powers our bodies right down to our cells. If you eat healthy, you encourage healthy cells and tissues to form, keeping your entire body healthy in return. When you eat healthy, you also promote healthy bodily functions.

For people with ADHD, certain foods have been shown to decrease the negative symptoms of ADHD. Eating plenty of protein is good for adults with ADHD because protein is filled with amino acids that help create neurotransmitters. Eat a lot of poultry, dairy, eggs, fish, beans, and nuts. Make sure you add plenty of zinc, magnesium, and iron to your diet too. These vitamins and minerals are present in lean meats, poultry, seafood, soy, nuts, and fortified cereals. Similarly, you need plenty of omega-3 fatty acids and B vitamins in your diet. They improve alertness and reduce symptoms of ADHD. This means you will need plenty of avocados, salmon, olive oil, winter squash, flaxseeds, and leafy greens in your diet. You will also need plenty of eggs, milk, liver (and other organ meats), yogurts, and legumes. Ginseng and ginkgo are known as "cognitive activators". They act like stimulants without the side effects of medication. They also reduce your impulsivity and increase your focus.

Avoid processed, high-sugar foods and caffeine, at all costs. They simply increase your hyperactivity, causing you to become restless. You should avoid artificial food dyes and preservatives too for the same reason.

For an adult with ADHD, your eating patterns may mirror your general behavior. For example, you may be impulsive and hyperactive in the way you eat, sometimes going without eating for many hours and then bingeing on whatever food you see around you. To manage ADHD, you need to plan and prepare your meals carefully to make sure you are receiving as many ADHD-beneficial nutrients as possible. If you are starving yourself only to binge on unhealthy foods, you are worsening your symptoms of ADHD and your emotional and physical health. It is best to plan your meals just as you plan other tasks in your life. That way, you will be sure to get plenty of nutrients at regular intervals.

Chapter Summary

- ADHD can make life very difficult for you when not treated.

- ADHD, when left unmanaged or untreated, can also significantly hurt the people around you and cause them serious problems, too.

- Regular exercising is a great way to manage the symptoms of ADHD.

- Regular exercise increases your mood, memory, concentration, focus, and motivation.

- To get better sleep, practice yoga and meditation an hour before bed every day.

- Certain foods have been proven to decrease the negative symptoms of ADHD.

Chapter Six: Self-Help and Alternative Strategies for Managing ADHD in Adults

Besides medical treatments, you can benefit from self-help and alternative strategies for managing your adult ADHD.

Horticultural Therapy/Gardening

Gardening and horticultural therapy have been scientifically proven to increase focus, calm the mind, and improve your emotional, physical, and mental health.

If you cannot have a garden, perhaps because of space or mobility issues, you can plant a few crops around the house, in hangers and pots placed on windowsills and tables. This will still produce the same effects as gardening. Remember that horticultural therapy does not mean just growing and tending to plants. It also means being among plants and even animals and nature. Visiting a farm or sitting on the beach near the trees to hear the ocean breeze will all produce the same calming effect. To learn more, visit the American Horticultural Therapy Association at: https://www.ahta.org/.

Mindfulness Meditation & Yoga

Regular mindfulness meditation and exercises that promote mindfulness and relaxation, such as yoga, have been proven to help clear the mind of unnecessary busyness, stress, and hyperactivity. These techniques help you activate your body's natural relaxation response and reverse the effect of stress that your ADHD may have on you. Likewise, they reduce the symptoms of anxiety and depression.

Other forms of exercise and stretching that enable mindfulness and relaxation, like tai chi and rhythmic exercise such as dancing, running, and swimming, are also just as beneficial. Lastly, you can give yourself regular self-massage to trigger the relaxation response in your body. Self-help strategies, although effective, work best when you pair them up with medication, so do not rely on ADHD management techniques solely as treatment.

Therapy

You can see a psychologist who specializes in ADHD for therapy and cognitive-behavioral therapy. Cognitive-behavioral therapy is therapy that seeks to change your cognitive, emotional, and behavioral patterns to bring you better health and a happier life.

Mental health professionals are highly trained to help you learn new skills that help you cope with your symptoms and change habits that are causing you problems.

Adults with ADHD often struggle with emotional and psychological issues and pain caused by their symptoms. For instance, patterns of academic and career difficulties and underachievement, failure, high job turnover, and relationship conflicts are common amongst people with ADHD. These issues can cause low self-esteem, shame, resentment, and a sense of "unworthiness" developed after years of criticism from loved ones. Seeking therapy can help you talk about this pain and learn alternative strategies to deal with it. You can also seek marriage and family counseling and therapy if your ADHD is causing significant troubles in your marriage and/or family relationships.

Professional Organizers

If your ADHD causes you to miss out on life because of your disorganization, you may hire a professional organizer to help you manage this area of your life. A professional organizer will help you develop an efficient organization system both at home (and in your personal life) and in the workplace. They also teach you how to manage your time and organize your life efficiently using ADHD-friendly methods.

Chapter Summary

- Gardening and horticultural therapy have been scientifically proven to improve the symptoms of ADHD.

- Mindfulness meditation and exercises that promote mindfulness are beneficial in improving ADHD symptoms.

- You can see a psychologist who specializes in ADHD for therapy and cognitive-behavioral therapy to help you talk about how ADHD affects your life, and they will help to develop strategies to assist you in managing your symptoms.

Final Words

Congratulations! You did it! Through reading this book you have taken a great first step towards lifelong healing.

Although it might be a challenge to have adult ADHD, you now have some more information on how ADHD is diagnosed, and what treatment methods you might like to pursue. You should now have a solid understanding of the treatment options available to you (both medical and traditional) and feel well-versed in how ADHD can be managed in adults. Finally, you are now armed with alternative and self-help strategies for managing your ADHD, including key facts on nutritional psychology and how diet can naturally reduce your symptoms.

Remember to always consult with a professional to receive an official diagnosis before beginning any treatment plan. Also remember that having ADHD isn't a bad thing – it just means your brain is wired a little differently than most. Finally, thanks for taking the time to read this book. I hope it has answered some questions and made the path forward a lot clearer for you!

References

Additude Editors. (2021). Why Sugar Is Kryptonite: ADHD Diet Truths. Retrieved from https://www.additudemag.com/adhd-diet-nutrition-sugar/.

Cathe. (2021). 5 Brain-Boosting Chemicals Released During Exercise. Retrieved from https://cathe.com/5-brain-boosting-chemicals-released-during-exercise/.

Demontis D., Walters, R.K., Martin J., Mattheisen M., Als T.D., Agerbo E., Baldursson G., Belliveau R., Bybjerg-Grauholm J., Bækvad-Hansen M., Cerrato F., Chambert K., Churchhouse C., Dumont A., Eriksson N., Gandal M., Goldstein J.I., Grasby K.L., Grove J., Gudmundsson O.O., Hansen C.S., Hauberg M.E., Hollegaard M.V., Howrigan D.P., Huang H., Maller J.B., Martin A.R., Martin N.G., Moran J., Pallesen J., Palmer D.S., Pedersen C.B., Pedersen M.G., Poterba T., Poulsen J.B., Ripke S., Robinson E.B., Satterstrom F.K., Stefansson H., Stevens C., Turley P., Walters G.B., Won H., Wright M.J.; ADHD Working Group of the Psychiatric Genomics Consortium (PGC); Early Lifecourse & Genetic Epidemiology (EAGLE) Consortium; 23andMe Research Team, Andreassen O.A., Asherson P., Burton C.L., Boomsma D.I., Cormand B., Dalsgaard S., Franke B., Gelernter J., Geschwind D., Hakonarson H., Haavik J., Kranzler H.R., Kuntsi J., Langley K., Lesch K.P., Middeldorp C., Reif A.,

Rohde L.A., Roussos P., Schachar R., Sklar P., Sonuga-Barke E.J.S., Sullivan P.F., Thapar A., Tung J.Y., Waldman I.D., Medland S.E., Stefansson K., Nordentoft M., Hougaard D.M., Werge T., Mors O., Mortensen P.B., Daly M.J., Faraone S.V., Børglum A.D., Neale B.M.. (2019). Discovery Of The First Genome-wide Significant Risk Loci For Attention Deficit/Hyperactivity Disorder. *Nat Genet.* 51(1), pp. 63-75.

Harvard Health Publishing. (2021). Exercise Is An All-Natural Treatment To Fight Depression. Retrieved from https://www.health.harvard.edu/mind-and-mood/exercise-is-an-all-natural-treatment-to-fight-depression.

LeMieux, J. (2018). ADHD's First Genetic Risk Variants Determined Through Large Genetic Study. Retrieved from https://www.genengnews.com/insights/adhds-first-genetic-risk-variants-determined-through-large-genetic-study/.

National Human Genome Research Institute. (2014). ADHD Genetic Research Study. Retrieved from https://www.genome.gov/Current-NHGRI-Clinical-Studies/ADHD-Genetic-Research-Study-at-NIH.

Newlifeoutlook. (2021). How And Why To Include Yoga In Your ADHD Management Plan. Retrieved from https://adhd.newlifeoutlook.com/yoga-adhd/.

Rones, N. (2021). Superfoods: The 19 Best Foods For Health And Happiness. Retrieved from https://time.com/collection/guide-to-happiness/4859607/superfoods-better-health/.

Smalley, S.L., Loo, S.K., Hale, T.S., Shrestha, A., McGough, J. Flook, L. and Reise, S. (2009). Mindfulness And Attention Deficit Hyperactivity Disorder. *Journal Of Clinical Psychology*. 65(10), pp. 1087-98.

CPSIA information can be obtained
at www.ICGtesting.com
Printed in the USA
LVHW051925270423
745523LV00002B/7

9 781959 018285